*the path that life takes
can be beautiful ...*

I believe that thoughts become things

I am a strong and grateful
woman. I feel peace, joy...

I AM A SEEKER OF ALL THINGS
MYSTERIOUS AND SPIRITUAL...

DARE TO DREAM, TAKE
RISKS, BE...

*I believe that making love creates the
greatest art on the canvas of our existence.*

The earth itself breathes; as do we...

Wise Women of a Mountain Village

A Celebration of the Women of Idyllwild, California

Judith Way

The Wise Woman stands out because she sees herself as a part of the whole.

She shines because she doesn't need to impress.

She achieves great things because she doesn't look for recognition.

Her wisdom is contained in what she is, not her opinions.

She refuses to argue; so no one argues with her.

~Lao Tzu

With Gratitude

I am feeling such a deep appreciation for all these amazing Idyllwild women who took the time for their photo shoots and their wise words. I am forever grateful, thank you.

I am so proud of Shelby our photographer. She worked her magic in the cold, heat, wind, altitude and the energy of many different women. Thank you Shelby. And to Jennifer, I am so thankful for your assistance to Shelby and me at these shoots.

A big thank you to Jim Crandall, my publisher who didn't mind all of my emails, texts and phone calls early and very late at times. You did a great job understanding my passion and my dream.

I would like to thank my mother for all of her help with the "small stuff" and the extra time she was able to spend with me.

A special thank you for my developmental editor, Margaret Curtis.

A great big thank you to Dori Capitani for letting us use his beautiful "heart" art work in Kelly's portrait on page 102.

I also want to thank Piper for ending this beautiful book with her words of love, healing, and expression of life "in the raw."

And I wish to thank my wonderful husband for being patient with me in times of complete chaos. I love you Robert!

I want to thank my favorite story teller and author, Clarissa Pinkola Estes for inspiring me with her sweet words of wisdom in the first paragraph

3

of my Prologue and also Joyce Tenneson for inspiring me with her first book of wisdom published back in 2002.

I would also like to thank Café Aroma, the Italian bistro in Idyllwild, where I have been able to create this book and other dreams that I have had come to fruition during my lunch breaks.

Thank you to Diana Syvertson, Peggy Durling, Sandi Fulcher, and Anne Finch for your seed offerings to help bring this book forward. I love you all!

And perhaps the most important: Our Heavenly Father for His gentle encouragements in the wee morning hours.

I am reminded of Rumi's words, "If you awake in the morning hours, DO NOT go back to sleep. It is in these hours that you are the closest to God."

So be it and so it is....

-*Judith Corrine Way*

O ne day, around the age of 45, I awoke as a wise woman. I can't remember the particular day, but it was a day when I decided that I would stop pleasing others and live for pleasing myself. I decided that what I thought really mattered. That day, I promised myself that I would stop caring so much what others thought of me; and I began to realize that it's really about me in this world. My happiness. My joy.

I remember feeling roots from my feet growing deeper in the earth as I grounded myself even more. I felt my heart becoming lighter and more open. My heartbeats seemed to ease. I can also recall my arms growing longer as if I were reaching around the world, aching to hug it. My arms were like the branches of the old wise oak tree … strong and ever so long. My legs felt thicker; toned and solid upon the earth. I looked into the mirror and stared at the woman with silvery-white long hair that used to be fiery-red. I looked deeper into my eyes and saw the little diamonds that replaced my tear ducts from the pressures of my world and the endless tears that I had shed for my friends and family. Now they shined with a brilliant light.

As I continued to look deeper into that mirror I saw that the deep lines and wrinkles in my face had grown beautiful rubies … brilliant and rich in color. The cracks in my lips, where there once were none, had little mirrors that reflected back on a life of bravery and forgiveness. Looking down a little further, I noticed that my breasts were not so perky; but full — full and heavy with the memories of nursing four strong sons, and loving three adventurous husbands. Yes, a wise woman. Me.

My story began over 20 years ago when a dear friend gave me the "Wise Women" book by Joyce Tenneson. I remember that after reading those beautiful words of insight by beautiful women of the world, I realized that I, too, have heard such amazing words coming from my fitness clients as they worked with me in their training hours. So began my journey with these books, from the communities in which I have lived.

Living here in Idyllwild, I have melded deeper into mother earth, making friends with our wildlife, talking to the birds and hugging our beautiful, thick, fragrant sugar pines. Ahhh, Idyllwild. What a sweet little Christmas town this is. Nestled in the San Jacinto Mountains above the Palm Springs desert. Famous for our nine wilderness trails, jazz music, "yummy" restaurants and art. If you haven't been here yet, you will. For this magical book, I asked the Idyllwild women to dig a little deeper with their words than my last book, Wise Women of a Small Village. They did, as you will read. Sixty-four courageous women stepped up to join me in this magical adventure. They will uplift you as they have me with their stories of challenges, triumphs and words of hope. I'm a little richer and wiser typing their words and assisting at their photo shoots. I am like a proud mother who has witnessed her daughters perform in a beautiful dance recital. Creating magic with Shelby, the photographer, and her assistant, Jenn; even inviting our publisher, Jim, to our last photo shoot. I wanted him to experience for himself how "Spirit" moves unexpectedly and surprises us with photos of grandiose exposures …

I wanted to bring you every season in Idyllwild, Winter, Spring, Summer and Fall. I feel these mountains are very healing. Just ask anyone who visits and lives here. I wanted to share our famous trails with you and our meadows, our music, our magic and our enchanting mountains. After all, this really is a celebration of all the women in our Idyllwild mountain community. And here they are, in all their glory. Sit back, take a deep breath. Enjoy. Perhaps you too might be inspired to write your own beautiful words on the page we left at the end of our book. May God bless you as He has all of us.

Judith Corrine Way

$\mathcal{O}$ver 50 years in Idyllwild, I still enjoy my work helping clients find their special homes. Raising our family, being involved in town events, I marvel at how easy it is to enjoy everyone on the Hill!

~ *Marge Muir*

I realize that life is about claiming who you are. It's about knowing yourself, expressing yourself and doing what makes you happy. IT'S REAL AND IT'S RAW. Even the dark night of our souls serves us. Choose to be happy and love with an open heart. Then your life will be full of love.

~ *Julie Bylli Johnson*

$\mathcal{I}$ believe in the power of nature, love, female energy, grace, gratitude and peace.

~ *Pam Goldwasser*

$\mathcal{I}$ am an EXTREMELY resourceful woman.

My gift is knowing how to help others.

I know just who to call, or where to go,

if you ever need my help.

~Chris Singer

$\mathcal{I}$ have learned that the only person who will meet my needs is Jesus.
He is my Prince, my Knight,

     my Rescuer, and my Redeemer. People have always
fallen short of my needs and expectations,

     except Him. "In all your ways acknowledge Him and He
will direct your path." — *Proverbs*

~Kimberly Ann Smith

$\mathcal{I}$am a 70 year old woman. When I was seven years old I made a decision that would affect the rest of my life in a way I could never have imagined. I grew up in post-war Germany, surrounded by devastation and overwhelming sadness. I told my mother that someday I would go to America. She laughed, so I saved every pfennig (penny) from whatever little money I was given or earned. At the age of 19, I had saved enough money and secretly learned some English, so was permitted to go to the USA for one year and stay with relatives in Ohio who had immigrated almost 100 years before. I was then invited to California to stay with an exchange student's family and get an education beyond the 8th grade. I met and married a very nice man who became my husband for almost 50 years. I earned my Master's Degree in Marriage and Family Therapy.

Together we have published many textbooks used for the training of counselors. I have been able to affect many people's lives, both with my writings as well as my teaching and counseling. I grew up in a small village, so I enjoy the small village of Idyllwild, where I have resided for 35 years. I have traveled to many places in the world, and it always feels good to return to Idyllwild. Remember not to give up on your dreams. Follow your passion and be open to meeting people who are different from you; they can teach you something. Embrace diversity, as it will make the world a more peaceful place.

~Marianne Schneider Corey

$\mathcal{W}$omen, we have several roles in our lives ... a daughter, a sister, a wife, a mother, a career woman, an empty-nester, a mentor, an old wizened woman, a dying woman. As women, our most challenging role is accepting each of these stages and gracefully moving, living and flourishing within them. If we don't, we feel unfulfilled. So let's wake up each day with a new resolve to find something good in it. Life is an ongoing daily challenge and the more we live within each day, the more we enjoy it.

~Maritha "Mimi" Lamp

The path that life takes can be beautiful and amazing

and it can also go through phases that are overwhelming and confusing

sometimes choices and decisions about your path can be clear and easy

other times they can be unclear and difficult

while it can be helpful to hear the perspective of others

learn to listen to yourself

trust your wisdom

listen to the silent whispers of your intuition

and let your intuition be your guide

~Julie Lively

Aging Isn't For Sissies!!!

I am a great grandmother of twins. I feel age is
only a number. Stay active and take good care of
your body. Stay true to your beliefs and you will see
that there is nothing you can't accomplish.

~Linda Rider

$\mathcal{I}$ am an artist, painter, pastelist and etcher. I am grateful to be on this adventure, living life with happiness and joy. I advise ... choose the high road.

~Joan Leal Carter

$\mathcal{I}$ believe that the USA is an American Dream for my people who have come here looking for a better way of life for our families. I am a strong, hard-working woman who is full of gratitude for all those people who have believed in me. I will always be grateful to God above for leading me in the right direction and putting me in the hands of caring and loving business owners here in Idyllwild.

~Lupita Montoya

Each and every girl possesses a voice within herself to make a difference in life and in her world. She simply needs to learn how to speak up and not be afraid to "Take Action." The smallest of actions can make a ripple that can change someone's entire life.

~Mary Frances Moore

I feel like a little girl, adolescent, and young woman — all inside my current self, in this place in time. I strive to use my wisdom, comprised of knowledge, intuition, and experience, to act with love.

~Dr. Brandi Kaye Davis Mills

We are in an incredible and unique period of time. Our soul is calling on us to release old programming which has kept us from who we really are. This task is not easy for the feminine vibration. Women's task right now is to change energetic patterns that do not come from loving ourselves and forgiving ourselves (and others). With practice, discipline and patience our consciousness grows and our heart expands. We begin to walk in our world in a new way on a level that we have only been able to imagine. We are the Way — Showers!

~ Celeste Mann

Things I learned on the mountain — Some people lose their way on the way to great things, be it a mountain peak or their life dreams. To get where you truly want to be, you must adventure boldly, but with purpose and forethought. Embrace change with flexibility and creativity, not fear. One thing you learn on a rescue mission — everything can change at a moment's notice. Tie yourself too tightly to a plan and you may miss a world of opportunity. Take care of yourself. Extreme self-sacrifice may bolster your ego, but unnecessarily overextending yourself will backfire at some point and can put all that you work for at risk. Ah, and to succeed? Meet challenges with focus, preparedness, creativity and confidence that you can and will do your best — be it on steep mountain slopes or on the journey towards your life goals.

~Helene Lohr

Wilderness Instructor, Search and Rescue

I am Dr. Judi. Idyllwild comes to me when they are in pain. I teach them that the world is full of spirit and grace and we only need to call upon it. What amazes me the most is that people take better care of their cars than they do their bodies. Don't they realize if they don't take care of themselves they won't need their cars?

~*Judi Milin*

$\mathcal{I}$ am a third generation Idyllwildian and a trail runner. I feel that growing up on this mountain is such a big part of who I am and continues to mold my person. Trail running has taught me many things, including patience with myself and the outside world. It has helped me feel a sense of awe for the ever-changing natural world, appreciation of my body and my mental and physical power, perseverance, and hope. Trail running is my therapy and my source of strength. Tread lightly, breathe deeply, and try to take it all in.

~Jana Baker

$\mathscr{I}$ am a particle of life and consciousness in this world. I feel a part of the Universe with every atom of my being. We who are conscious, are the eyes of the Universe and it manifested us in order to understand itself! That is exactly how I feel. I like understanding the incredible miracle of being on this Blue Planet in the Orion arm of the Milky Way, and our place in this vast and wondrous Cosmos. As an artist, my mission in this life is to beautify the world one brushstroke at a time.

~Svetlana E. Lustig

$\mathcal{W}$elcome Home

Mountain cabin nest

sp quiet — nature's welcome

Among trees, peace, joy

$\mathcal{I}$dyllwild

Our town — saved from fire

Our community grateful

Love heals and new growth

~$\mathcal{D}$enise $\mathcal{D}$iamond

I believe that thoughts become things ... and I have cultivated that awareness. I am quick to banish negative thoughts (and sometimes, people), focusing my precious time and energy on love, gratitude and following my dreams. I am grateful to be living the life of my dreams right here in Idyllwild. It was no accident.

~Kathy Harmon-Luber

$\mathcal{W}$hen disease enters your life, be it physical or environmental, it also brings you gifts.

You learn the strengths of yourself and the people around you. You have a chance to live a life well lived.

As Maya Angelou says,

"When you know better, you do better"

~*Grace Reed*

$\mathcal{I}$ am the Huggin' Banker on "The Hill" who advocates

for education and the environment. I have a special focus on

advancing the status of women and girls throughout the world.

My advice is to "Always give service to others. And always take the

high road, even if you have to put it in 4-wheel drive!"

~Jeri Sue Haney

IDYLLWILD Garden Club 19

$\mathcal{I}$ feel we are all here for a purpose. Our divine positioning has caused our paths to cross. It is our quest to love, to share, to give, to teach and to learn from each other. And through this quest, we become sisters for life.

~Lisa Furugen

Treasure the wonder revealed in the natural world

the shimmering reflective water

the vast spacious sky

the song of a bird on the wing

the breeze in the trees

the falling leaves

a butterfly

the buzzing bees

Recognizing our oneness with the earth and our natural wisdom held in the sacred temple of the body. Breathe deep and tend the inner flame of your open heart. Seeing through the innocent eyes of the magical child. Explore, discover, create, laugh and play with abandon. Cultivate gratitude and generosity. Recognizing our reflection in the mirror of each and every being ... LOVE and listen deeply. Knowing you are radiant light.

~Jennifer McEwen

"Be here now." That's all we need to know, really. We are all in this together, and Idyllwild is the perfect place to come, shed noise and the confusion of the world, and let in only what you want to let in.

~Laurie Gillett

$\mathcal{D}$ear Mila,

Even though you are not born yet, I want to share with you all the things it has taken me 54 years to learn. Perhaps I can save you a little heartache.

"GMA'S PEARLS OF WISDOM"~

     *Learn something new every day.

     *Challenge yourself, don't play it safe. Fear can be a good thing.

     *You will read all kinds of tales of one true love and Prince Charming. They are all believable. Well, there are so many kinds of love ...

     *Friends come in all ages, shapes and colors. Don't miss an opportunity to make or be a friend.

     *Touch is magical ...

P.S. Open letter

Love You Already, Gma

~GiGi Kramer

Treat the Earth and all that dwell therein with respect. Remain close to the Great Spirit. Show great respect for your fellow beings and work together for the benefit of all Mankind. Look after the well-being of your Mind and Body and always be truthful and honest. And always remember to take full responsibility for your own actions.

~Diane Miller

♪♪ *W*hen you are frightened and you want to hide

All of your feelings are mixed up inside

Try to see calmly, rather than fight

It'll be all right, it'll be all right ♪♪

~*Elaine Balkman Latimer*

I've learned to put
my arms around myself and
say, "I love you."

I am stronger, wiser and more joyful as I live more years on this planet. I believe that my body is a vessel of God, and it is up to me to keep it healthy, strong and full of love.

~Maureen McElligott

I know for certain that things WILL change. They must!
You can always count on that.

~Anne Finch

I greatly treasure friends and family. I believe that helping to make others' lives better is extremely important. I hope my life will make a positive difference in that direction. Make yourself happy. No one else is responsible for you, except you.

~Suzon Montelius Capparelli

Avatar's Enlightened Liberation

Element benders

Bone menders

Light tenders

Are we

When you can do

All these things

Then you'll be

Set free

~T Qi

(Teresa Halliburton)

Art can be a lifeline. I grew up in a strict military family where physical beatings and verbal putdowns were the norm. I developed low self-esteem and couldn't form lasting relationships. But God didn't turn his back on me. He gave me art. It has helped me to heal and reach out to a better world. I paint portraits of jazz legends like Billie Holiday, Ella Fitzgerald and Etta James because their lives were worse than mine. And where would the world be without their incredible voices? If you've had a bad childhood, remember that you are not broken. You can use your art to heal, criticize, honor, and yes, even change the world!

~Marcia Gawecki

My wisdom to you is to never go anywhere empty handed. And I also invite you to remember, "Someone knows the answer to your question — your job is to find them." I feel truly blessed in these mountains and I believe in my life.

~Karen Doshier

$\mathcal{I}$ am caught up in the beauty of Tahquitz ... the movement heavenward ... as I gaze into the stars ... I feel called to this mountain, overpowered by Love-Light. Called to be a Nun ... singing wonder, gratitude and praise. The stones are alive and bid us climb into the heavens and become a dancing star. "Be still and know I am God." Serenity smiles upon the mountain ... at the vortex of wonder and spiritual energy I have been gifted to pray and offer the bread and wine of thanksgiving.

~Sister Rosemarie Sunbeam Dancing

Curiosity is a great human trait—probably essential to the evolution of humans. To be curious is to explore—to wonder—to be full of Wonder, to imagine. Curiosity leads us to appreciation. To appreciate differences, how the world around us works, how the stars hang in the sky, how invisible particles move through the universe and are essential to life. To appreciate that people can cry at the happiest moments and find a moment to laugh during the saddest. Without curiosity, how would storytelling come about? Our ancestors created legends explaining the curious aspects of nature. Curiosity can feed your imagination every day.

~Anne Erikson

There is such a unique joy in helping a woman bring her inner beauty out that may have been buried for a long time. It gives my heart such happiness if I can help bring out a woman's natural beauty that God gave her, enhancing it with natural looking color, and then the right applications to make her blossom into a creature of more loveliness in a very little bit of time. The second greatest commandment in the Bible is to LOVE OUR NEIGHBORS AS OURSELVES and with your inner beauty intact, you can obey that commandment even better than before.

~Angela Colson

*I*dyllwild is my creative and spiritual home, a place of profound healing.

Living here among the giving pines and walking this sacred labyrinth have slowed me to the inner knowing of Spirit.

From this stillness, I heard Spirit calling me forth to my lineage of healers in Bulgaria, the wisdom of my bones, and the platform of women who came before me.

I am the living torch bearer of that wisdom. When I write, I feel the pure joy that comes from unleashing it upon the page.

My words light the way for my daughters and future granddaughters to tap into their own limitless reservoir of wisdom.

~Denise McGregor

$\mathcal{I}$am a woman who embraces change, truth, growth, evolution of self and soul while being deeply grounded into the Heart of Mother Earth and filled by the Breath of Great Spirit. Step out of the matrix and go deep inside, face your inner shadow, shadow dance, and take time to know yourself.

~ *Careena Chase*

$\mathcal{I}$feel blessed. I am able to express my inner self by playing music. Music has brought me through some tough times. Music has the power to connect and bring people together from different backgrounds, walks of life and cultures.

~Sandii Castleberry Daigh

I am a Lady of the Mountain

I feel gratitude opens our hearts to the beauty all around us.

It gives us the courage to let go and trust.

It lovingly helps us connect with ourselves, others, and God.

With a grateful heart we are able to see that every day is a gift filled
with possibility and every challenge an opportunity for growth.

When love moves through us it inspires all we do.

Never underestimate the healing power of a simple gift
given with love. Your offering may be someone's saving grace.

I walk the sacred path of healing with grace, beauty, and
gentleness. In my medicine basket I carry a mother's prayers,
flowers, sage, and gratitude.

~Denise Foshay Gioeli

Circa 1996, I had a dream. I was dancing with the Buddha Christ. I love Jesus but I also love the wisdom of Buddha. Which I call the "Buddha Christ." And he said, "See how easy this is? Trust, relax, allow ... " as we danced into the light.

~Dr. Susan Foster

$\mathcal{B}$e Humble. Be Grateful. Be Kind. Surround yourself with people who love you, inspire you and challenge you. Never stop listening and learning.

*L*et the beauty and majesty of the Idyllwild Mountains be a constant reminder to you of the ever-present God who created it.

~Sandy Browning

$\mathcal{I}$am a seeker of all things mysterious and spiritual. Life is such a gift. There is so much to learn ... to see ... to feel ... and to create. Being free in your own spirit is the key to inner serenity. Trusting yourself ... really hearing yourself is essential. Letting go of old scars ... remembering the lesson ... forgiveness of others and yourself. Humanity errs and from those errs ... we grow. We wouldn't be "Wise" without many exceptional experiences ... get out and LIVE!

~Kirsten Ingbretsen

*I*dyllwild is a special place that allows you to be whatever
you want to be ...

~Kate Sirkin

$\mathcal{I}$ am a strong and grateful woman. I feel peace,
joy and happiness. I believe you should always
follow your heart and you WILL live the life
of your dreams.

~ *Sandi Fulcher*

Chase your dreams. No matter who you are or where you're from, your dreams are just as relevant and valuable as you are.

~Samantha Hallaun

$\mathcal{I}$am made from the same material as the stars. I am part of a magnificent creation. I love music and art ... never regret spending money on either!

Support an artist. It is a gift that will bless both of you.

~Kelly Visel

*M*y Insight?

Most people haven't any inkling of what it's like to finally discover who you are, only to find that you're living in the wrong kind of body.

Can you really imagine that?

~Regina Caron

I feel the beauty of nature that surrounds me and I understand its purpose. I am passionate, strong and a true believer of giving to others. I am blessed. I thank God for all of His blessings. I believe there's a time for everything. Work hard, love a lot and never give up. Treasure your memories and remember, women are amazing! Believe in your powerful self and search your soul. Find out what makes you feel at peace with yourself. Then you'll know your true self.

~Suesen Angevine

$\mathcal{I}$ love the Lord God with my whole heart, mind and soul. I love my husband as God's precious gift to me. Loving unconditionally, joyfully, honestly and openly is the key to a happy marriage. I learned that from Jesus, my parents and my husband. When I love that way, I am loved that way. We will celebrate forty-six years of marriage in June.

~Peggy Durling

$\mathcal{I}$ believe that someday, women will one day, again, rule the world ...

~ *Laurie Hidy*

$\mathcal{I}$dyllwild is a little slice of heaven. A place where I can relax and get away from the chaos of the city. A place to gather myself and become the adventurous woman I am. On to photographing!

~*Pamela Lagoni*

I believe that all women arrive on this planet filled with beauty. I am reminded of what Emerson said, "All we must do is release our impersonal splendor."

~Phyllis Curington-Brown

I've spent much of my life around children. My own five. My hundreds of students over the years. The wisdom I've gained? I'm thinking of those who have influenced me with their words. And I wonder: have I graced my children's lives or my students' lives with such wisdom? As a wife, mother, educator, and friend, I try to remember these wise words:

Courage

Patience

Vision

Hope

Be kind.

Be remarkable.

Be.

~Sally Salter

I cherish everybody and every child that I have embraced. They make me grateful for my past and hopeful for their future. I pray they know how much they've touched my life and I hope I have enriched their future.

~*Georgianna "Gege" Lee Beagle*

118

I am a woman and in my journey I have learned the lesson that even the darkest day has its bittersweet song. I believe there is a bond, like a heartbeat, between loss and victory, between singing and weeping, between losing and healing. And the lesson of love is most important of all.

~Wendi Strebe

You meet the love of your life the day you are born.
You might spend a portion of your life searching for this <u>love</u>,
until you <u>realize</u> that what you had been searching for that whole
time had been yourself. Don't waste your life running circles
around your<u>self</u>. Find <u>LOVE</u> now, let go of false realities and
<u>receive</u> all you are! Just be.

(Note: Meditate on underlined words)

~Sarah Spencer

I believe in rising — I believe in song and sacred dance — I believe in love, and pain, and tears, and earth, and children, and dreaming, and Dr. Seuss worlds. I believe in healing and forgiveness and expression of experience. I believe in silence — in season — in GOD. I believe in life. I believe that I am ever-changing the depth and clarity of my beliefs.

I believe in life. I believe in the call of the coyote and the rhythm of the eagles' flight. I believe in the whispers of the lakes and the lies of the snow fall. I believe that making love creates the greatest art on the canvas of our existence. I believe in red wine, tear-filled midnights before a raging fire. I believe in Andrea Bocelli and the camp fire guitar strings. I believe that faith spawns strength and regret spawns death. I believe in yesterday, today and tomorrow. I believe in the roses' fragrance as a bud and as fallen petal. I believe in my daughters and in their seeds of promise.

~Piper Dellums

I am an evolving and transforming spiritual woman of grace, compassion and love. I believe that solitude is a precious gift to ourselves. Seek out older wise women. Listen to them tell their stories of strength, determination and peace. Remember your girlfriends always ... we are a powerful force on this earth.

~Iva Zander Botton

$\mathcal{B}$reathe

The earth itself breathes; as do we.

Nature is the touchstone of wakening spirit and healing.
Seek the Divine in solitude. Be still often. It nourishes, heals
and replenishes. Lie on a rock and let the sun and wind take
inventory of you. Write, in order to read prophecy. Listen to your
body; trust your intuition. Be strong as steel and as formative as
running waters. Walk daily in deepest gratitude. Laugh often and
authentically; it is the best way to breathe. Daydream, bust clouds
and learn how to ask for help.

The earth itself breathes; as do we.

~Margaret Di Zinno
It'll Be All Right

My Wisdom

About the Author

A mother of four handsome sons — Joshua, Brandon, Austin and Cory, "Grami" to nine beautiful grandchildren, and wife of California State Parks Ranger Robert Peek, Judith is a published author and personal fitness trainer with 35 years of experience, now specializing in Pilates and CranioSacral Therapy. She is a lover of life, the human body, Harley Davidson motorcycles, Jesus, and of course, chocolate. She is constantly learning, evolving, and growing, spiritually and intellectually. She lives a peaceful yet busy life in Idyllwild, California.

About the Photographer

$\mathscr{P}$hotographer, Shelby Houskeeper, has been a portrait and graphic artist since 2001. Working with her father in their third generation family studio in Fallbrook, California has provided her with a comfortable creative working environment. On-the-job training by her father, as well as workshops and seminars, has given Shelby a wide variety of portrait experience. Family, Children's Portraits, and Weddings are all areas of photography she enjoys. However, High School Senior Portraits are a favorite for her. Beginning with hand printing in a darkroom to the current digital enhancements, she has enjoyed the journey of learning. The opportunity to work with Judith on the Idyllwild book has been a unique adventure.

Epilogue

We are stepping into the vast ocean of wisdom, each and every day, moment by moment, from the rise of the SUN/SON to the going down of the same. We are seeking the origin of our sacred wisdom — our purpose and promise from teary midnight reflections, to the shadows of yesterday's dawn.

Wisdom is a poem written on the spirit and flesh of life unfolding. We bleed like a virgin or a man in the killing fields. We know the metallic scent of the escaping of life very well. It perfumes our walk, like expensive perfume and drying branches of sage. We love with abandon freely, awkwardly without boundary or distinction. Our love has given us the greatest pleasures and the deepest sorrows of this life ... and yet we still believe in love. We laugh until it hurts and cry until it no longer does.

Wisdom is a poem that will never be completed, a mosaic of the fragility and brilliance of the broken and mended pieces of our lives. We are just one temporary song of the ages, passing as quickly as thought and young love into nostalgia, into forever, into forgetfulness, into history. We transcend and grow with the ebb and flow of the seasons. We are cleansed and made still in the fingers of rain storms. We are Phoenix on the rise, pressing through the frozen barren earth of winter's dread and winter's beauty.

We are survivors. We are the promising and budding birth of spring awakening beneath the icy feet of trauma, illness, insanity, genius, compassion, love, lost-love, given love and love birthed. If you are truly listening, even in the silence and secrets of ours, you will hear the composition of our every breath. We will give our last drop of life to our children, our community, a stranger, a nation, and GOD. We are survivors, worshipers, mothers, and scarred, shattered masterpieces of distinction.

We are clarity and hypocrisy, stunningly ugly and oh so beautiful. We are fame and fortune. Poverty and elusiveness, desperation and contentment. Seen, but invisible, bigger than life, but smaller than atom/ADAM. We are supported by the rock of ages, yet we are scarred. We feel that the rock of Idyllwild sustains us yet it overwhelms us. Some of us have been called here to Idyllwild to heal and even to die ...

We are women, we are scarred, we are aging, like the wilting mountain rose bushes. We are ethnicity, we are intimate expression and insecure flesh. We are life. LIFE IS EVERYTHING. We fear life more than we fear death and yet, we have no fear. We ARE and that has to be enough as the wisdom of ourselves exists. We continue on the path set before us and then, we will no longer be here but there where we belong. Hold us down, like a ravenous lover. In this photographic moment press us as flowers into the album of time that represents NOW. See us in the light; for tomorrow, who knows what the eye of the sky will create in all of us here on these pages.

I AM ... WE ARE ... EVE

~Piper Dellums

Library of Congress Control Number: 2014931283

ISBN: 978-1-631-73928-6

Judith Way - Author
P.O. Box 524
Idyllwild, CA 92549
www.wisewomenof.com
Email: judiway2020@gmail.com
(760) 535-3852

Ahrend Studios - Photographer
211 East Alvarado Street
Fallbook, CA 92028
www.ahrendstudios.com
Phone: (760) 728-7613

Jim Crandall - Publisher
Idyllwild Publishing
P.O. Box 1313
Idyllwild, CA 92549
www.idyllwildpublishing.com
Email: jim.crandall@verizon.net
Phone: (951) 265-5732

Idyllwild Publishing
Websites & Graphic Design

I am made from the same material as the stars...

One day women will, once again, rule the world...

Each and every girl possesses a voice within herself...

I believe in song and sacred dance...

I realize that life is about claiming who you are...

Be as strong as steel and as formative as running waters...